How to Dry Herbs

The Ultimate Guide to Easily Drying Herbs at Home

Ella Marie

© 2015 Sender Publishing

© Copyright 2015 by Sender Publishing - All rights reserved.

This document is geared towards providing exact and reliable information in regards to the topic and issue covered. The publication is sold with the idea that the publisher is not required to render accounting, officially permitted, or otherwise, qualified services. If advice is necessary, legal or professional, a practiced individual in the profession should be ordered.

From a Declaration of Principles which was accepted and approved equally by a Committee of the American Bar Association and a Committee of Publishers and Associations.

In no way is it legal to reproduce, duplicate, or transmit any part of this document in either electronic means or in printed format. Recording of this publication is strictly prohibited and any storage of this document is not allowed unless with written permission from the publisher. All rights reserved.

The information provided herein is stated to be truthful and consistent, in that any liability, in terms of inattention or otherwise, by any usage or abuse of any policies, processes, or directions contained within is the solitary and utter responsibility of the recipient reader. Under no circumstances will any legal responsibility or blame be held against the publisher for any reparation, damages, or monetary loss due to the information herein, either directly or indirectly.

Respective authors own all copyrights not held by the publisher.

The information herein is offered for informational purposes solely, and is universal as so. The presentation of the information is without contract or any type of guarantee assurance.

The ideas, concepts and/or opinions delivered in this book are to be used for educational purposes only. This book is provided with the understanding that authors and publisher are not rendering medical advice of any kind, nor is this book intended to replace medical advice, nor to diagnose, prescribe or treat any disease, condition, illness or injury.

It is imperative that before beginning any diet or exercise program, including any aspect of this book, you receive full medical clearance from a licensed doctor and/or physician. Author and publisher claim no responsibility to any person or entity for any liability, loss, or damage caused or alleged to be caused directly or indirectly as a result of the use, application or interpretation of the material in this book.

The trademarks that are used are without any consent, and the publication of the trademark is without permission or backing by the trademark owner. All trademarks and brands within this book are for clarifying purposes only and are owned by the owners themselves, not affiliated with this document.

For more books by this author, please visit
www.wellnessbooks.net

Table of Contents

Introduction 1
Chapter 1: Why Drying Herbs is Important 3
Chapter 2: Picking Herbs to Dry 8
Chapter 3: Preparing for the Drying Process 12
Chapter 4: Drying Methods 17
Chapter 5: How to Store Dried Herbs 23
Chapter 6: Common Mistakes to Avoid 27
Chapter 7: Common Herbs to Dry 32
Conclusion 38

Introduction

It is no secret that herbs have been used for nutritional value and medicinal purposes for millennia. The fact that they are still used in countless civilizations around the world attests to their health benefits. At the supermarket, however, you can end up paying high costs for fresh herbs of questionable quality.

You can never really know what you're getting. Some online websites claim that they have the *best quality*. But according to whom? How do you know the truth, when some online businesses are honest, while others are just trying to turn a high profit from your ignorance. Finding the best deal and the best quality is difficult, if not impossible.

An alternative to buying herbs, however, is growing your own and then harvesting them. They are fun to grow and don't cost much. They don't even require much care, and then they're available for you to use whenever you are ready. In this book you will learn about harvesting, drying, and storing your herbs so that they can later be cooked with and served.

To grow herbs, you don't need much room, as it doesn't take a full-scale garden. You can decide to grow the herbs outdoors, but they would even fit on the windowsill in your kitchen. You won't have to dedicate tons of time to taking care of them either.

You will, however, need to invest some time and energy into starting the plants off right. They need the right amount of water and sunlight. You'll also need to occasionally prune them, so that the dead foliage doesn't steal vital nutrients from the healthy plant.

The drying process itself is also very important to understand. If the herbs aren't properly dried, they can grow moldy and become ruined. Improperly dried herbs also won't offer the same value you want or expect.

Now, you may be acknowledging the value of herbs, but insisting that you couldn't grow them yourself. Too often, people shy away from something new. Instead, you should be bold and embrace this opportunity. Starting is the first step toward achieving all the benefits. The choice is yours.

Furthermore, it isn't difficult to dry herbs, and this book will help you explore plenty of options. The method you choose to use often comes down to personal preference. Or, you may wish to try a few options and see what fits best with your needs.

You don't need to be an expert to grow and dry your own herbs. However, you do need to have a basic understanding of the steps involved. Proper storage is just as important as drying the herbs. The key is to have the herbs ready for use whenever you want them.

You will be very happy with the results from growing and drying your own herbs. You'll know the exact ingredients, nutritional values, and medicinal purposes. When so many store-bought items are treated with chemicals and pesticides, home-grown foods can also provide you with some peace-of-mind.

Chapter 1
Why Drying Herbs is Important

Drying herbs properly is important so they don't lose their nutritional or medicinal values. It doesn't make any sense to take the time to grow and harvest them, but then drop the ball when it comes to drying and storing.

Prevention

Preventing mold, yeast, and bacteria from growing on your herbs is essential. This can only be accomplished by removing all of the moisture from them. Unfortunately, moisture can't be seen, but its presence will soon be known: when you open a jar or a bag of your dried herbs, they will be ruined. The color and smell will immediately indicate if something isn't right. When you dry them completely, however, you won't have that issue.

Accessibility

It can be virtually impossible to always have fresh herbs around. They don't last for very long. However, when you dry them, they'll be ready for your use at any time. You can quickly access them from your home instead of rushing out to the store in search of fresh herbs.

You will also feel good knowing that they were grown without chemicals. You can't know this for sure when you buy dried herbs from a company. If you want something that's all natural, it's best to be assured of its origins.

Ideally, you should grow enough herbs to get you through the fall and winter months. By doing this, you can have enough until the spring when you will start over with growing and harvesting new ones. Don't store dried herbs for more than a year as they will start to lose their overall value. It can be hard at first to estimate how much you will use over a year, but do your best to judge.

Pay attention to how much and frequently you use herbs now, and during your first year, so you can adjust for the future. If you need more, it's best to keep various plants at different stages of growth. Then you don't have to start all over and wait before you have more of the herb available.

Cost

You will spend significantly less drying your herbs than you will buying them. In fact, you will spend less on the entire process of growing them, harvesting them, drying them, and storing them, than you will buying them.

If you use herbs often, this will save you money and makes a lot of sense. As you learn more about the health benefits different herbs offer, you will be inclined to use them even more than you do right now. Saving money is a bonus you don't want to pass up.

Additionally, what if you develop a chronic health problem due to poor nutrition? You'll end up spending even more on doctor visits, co-pays, deductibles, and medications. Many herbs actually help prevent illness, and that can add up to more money staying in your pocket.

Health Benefits

Different types of herbs offer either nutritional or medicinal value. Some of them offer both! It is important to understand these attributes when considering growing, harvesting, drying, and storing them.

Spend some time reading information and case studies from reputable books or websites. You'll learn that, time and time again, the results indicate that consumption of various herbs makes people feel better and reduces their symptoms of any health problems.

The world of modern medicine may not fully understand the use of herbs—yet—but they can't ignore the value that they offer. It's also a fact that for centuries, our ancestors relied on herbs and natural remedies for survival.

When you use herbs as directed, there is no health risk to you. When it comes to extracting oils from herbs, remember that they are quite potent. Just a few drops will go a long way! With all of this in mind, you have nothing to lose by giving herbs a try.

Nutritional Value

Many people cook with herbs because they like their flavors. However, these tastes developed because the ingredients offered nutritional value.

Our ancestors didn't eat processed foods or large amounts of sugar, and they engaged in physical work day after day for survival. The foods they ate were chosen to offer them the best nutritional value. This was not only to fit their bodies' needs, but to reduce the risk of health problems as well.

Cinnamon, for example, can help increase the metabolism. Consequently, it regulates blood sugar levels. This is especially true for people who experience a significant spike in blood sugar level after meals.

Dried cloves, on the other hand, offer powerful antioxidants. They help reduce the risk of various health concerns, and can prompt your body to function at its very best.

These are just a few of the examples of how herbs can help you to feel much better, in addition to enhancing the taste of your foods. We all must eat, so why not eat something that's healthy and tasty?

Medicinal Value

Dried ginger powder is naturally anti-inflammatory and is a prime example of an herb with great medicinal value. It can help to reduce the pain and discomfort that is often associated with various forms of arthritis.

With all of the great information out there, more people are inclined to use dried herbs for medicinal value. This can help them to avoid the cost of expensive medications. It can also help them avoid the harsh side effects from such medications.

However, this doesn't mean that the use of dried herbs is a substitute for medical care. You should be careful not to diagnose and treat yourself or others. Always work with your medical professionals to assess and treat health concerns.

Don't be shy about telling your doctor that you use herbs for medicinal purposes either. Though they won't often prescribe herbs specifically, they also shouldn't tell you not to use them. It is important to always be honest with your doctor so they know what you are consuming and how often.

Keep in mind that many cultures survived for hundreds of years by relying on herbs. They didn't have hospitals and other facilities where they could go for care like we do today. Many consumers like the idea of "going back to the basics" and avoiding pharmaceutical drugs.

There are some general rules you need to follow if you plan to grow and harvest herbs for medicinal purposes. They are:

- Growing the right herbs for your health needs.

How to Dry Herbs

- Making sure the soil in which you plant them isn't full of harmful chemicals.
- Picking your herbs midmorning or early afternoon so the dew has evaporated. (Dew will increase the risk of mold.)

Chapter 2
Picking Herbs to Dry

Once you have decided which herbs to grow, you need to follow the instructions for them carefully. Some will require more water or sunlight than others. Pay attention to the way they look and change your care routine if things aren't going well.

Label your herbs, too, when you plant them, because so many look alike once they start to grow. You need to be confident about what a given herb is before you use it for its nutritional value or medicinal purposes.

It's also important to keep a good eye on the foliage of the herbs as they grow. Take the time to weed them and to remove any parts of the plants that look damaged or diseased. If you see that the stem is discolored, the foliage is drooping, or the plant has black spots, you know you have an issue that can't be ignored.

Some herbs need to be pulled while others need to be cut. There are also those that need to be plucked. Using the proper method is important so you don't damage or ruin what you harvest. You will need sharp knives and sharp scissors to do the job correctly.

Use the Entire Plant

Don't automatically toss out the plant and use only its roots. Only certain types of herbs operate that way. Make sure you have the right information for the herbs you are working with. The way to harvest one herb may not be the best for the next.

Select the leaves that look the healthiest to harvest. The older leaves aren't going to offer you as much value. You can collect them and use them as mulch for your yard so they don't go to waste. Depending on the herbs you're growing, you may be using:

- leaves
- stems
- seeds
- flower-heads
- bark
- roots

When to Harvest

Knowing when to cut and harvest the herbs can be intimidating at first. If you are too early, your yield can be too small; if you are too late, the plants may be damaged. Growing them indoors in small pots is the easiest way to keep a good eye on them.

Each herb varies in when it is ready to be harvested. This means you need to become familiar with the details of the particular herbs you are growing. When you first start out, stick to no more than three herbs. This will let you focus on them without feeling overwhelmed.

As your level of comfort and expertise grows, you can begin to plant more herbs . You'll want to get the basics down and manage your time, however. Otherwise, all of the work you put into growing them will be a waste.

Quite a few herbs that people grow are leafy plants that will yield seeds. Once the seeds have developed, the plants won't continue to grow. They have served their intended purpose. Pick the leaves often to encourage more foliage to grow before those seeds appear. Such herbs include basil, chives, and parsley.

Basil needs to be cut frequently during the growing process. If you allow it to grow untamed, it gets stretched out. When you trim it, you will notice that the plant grows outwards as well as upwards. It also becomes a very deep green color. It is ready to harvest when it is about 12" tall and has several green leaves.

Chives tend to grow very quickly. They mainly grow in the spring and summer. If you use them often, plant them in various pots at different times. This allows you to harvest and dry some, while others are still growing and will be ready to harvest in a few weeks.

Parsley can be very tricky to cut when it is ready to harvest. Grab the entire leaf and hold it around the stalk. Nip it at the area where it begins to clump. The older leaves are tough, so avoid cutting them.

You will need to harvest rosemary before it becomes woody. Trim the shoots but don't cut into the branches that are woody and lacking leaves. You can dry rosemary in bunches, so don't worry if you harvest quite a bit of it at once.

The best way to harvest basil is with scissors that are held tightly between the thumb and finger. Snip right above a pair of leaves where you can see new growth. If you cut below a leaf, the stem will be too short for it to continue to grow. Instead, it will wither away and you will have to replace it.

Capsicum should be cut when it changes colors. Many people cut it when it is still green. However, if you are patient, it will start to turn yellow, red, and orange. That is when you should harvest it. You must be very careful with the stems as they are quite brittle.

Mint is one of the easiest herbs to grow and to harvest. Snip from healthy, mature leaves. This will allow it to continue to grow and for you to harvest more when you need it.

Oregano has very shallow roots so you need to be careful with them. This is one of the few herbs where you are encouraged to snip the older leaves and use them. Allow the younger leaves to remain in place so they can continue to grow and flourish.

How to Dry Herbs

With sage, snip the younger leaves that are still tender. However, you don't want to cut more than half of the plant. If you do, it won't produce new leaves for you anymore. Try to harvest it early in the day when the leaves are dry from the dew. However, don't wait until it gets too hot or the essential oils will be dried out by the heat of the sun.

Thyme is another herb with very shallow roots, so you need to harvest it with care. Use a pair of scissors to gently remove what you need. Take care not to use too much force or you will uproot the entire plant.

When you harvest shallots, cut from the outside and work your way in. You will see the center of the plant has new shoots emerging. They will replace those outer leaves you cut away.

This is hardly an exhaustive list, so don't worry if you don't see instructions for the herbs you are interested in growing. A little research online will tell you the best methods for growing and harvesting other herbs. You can also watch step-by-step videos online, which can be very helpful when you first start to grow your own herbs.

Chapter 3
Preparing for the Drying Process

The items you need to prepare for the drying process really depend on the method you use. Don't worry, none of them require buying expensive equipment or anything like that. Most people have almost everything they need already in their home.

Time

Time is essential for drying herbs, because you can't rush the process. You need to successfully dry the herbs the right way. It you aren't willing to allow this time, there is no point in even starting. Keep in mind that the process may take longer the first few times you harvest. After that, you will be able to do it faster and more efficiently.

Supplies

The supplies you will need depends on the method you plan to use for the drying. You will read about these options in a future chapter and can decide then.

If you are going to hang the herbs to dry, you will need twine.

You will also need burlap sacks or cheese cloth. These items are to cover the herbs so the sunlight won't rob them of their value. The UV rays helps them dry, but too much exposure reduces the overall potency of the herbs.

If you are going to use the oven, you will need several baking sheets. This allows you to put the herbs in a single layer. You can use a dehydrator with trays or your microwave.

Some people like to use gloves so they aren't touching the herbs directly. Get disposable gloves so you can take them on and off throughout the process as you need to. You can get a package of disposable gloves for just a few dollars.

Packaging and Labeling

You will also need bags or jars for storing dried herbs successfully. They should also be labeled. This will be covered in more depth in a future chapter.

You don't need large jars unless you plan to use the herbs in large amounts. You can get small glass jars that have cork lids. These look great and they don't take up much space. You can easily label them and keep them accessible.

Work Area

You will need plenty of work space in order to successfully harvest your herbs. A kitchen counter or kitchen table is a great option. Make sure everything is wiped down and dried before you start working with the herbs.

If you are using a method of drying that will take several weeks, you'll need to keep that space undisturbed for the required amount of time. It is this issue with the space that often encourages people to use faster herb drying methods, such as the oven or dehydrator.

However, when hanging to dry, they won't take up much space at all. You will need your work area again, though, when they are completely dry. This is when you are going to crumble them and package them.

Washing and Cleaning

You need to wash the herbs that you have harvested before you dry them. Use a brush with stiff bristles to gently remove any residue or soil. A nail brush is ideal because it is small and fits snuggly around your fingers for a good grip.

Rinse off the residue and dirt with warm water. Carefully pat dry with paper towels to remove the excess water. You can also allow the herbs to dry on a towel on the counter while you are working with others.

Some consumers skip this washing part of the process. They figure it will make the herbs take longer to dry. However, if you don't wash them, you risk dirt and residue getting into your food when you cook with them.

The washing doesn't take more than a few minutes, and you can gently pat the herbs dry with paper towels. Don't skip this step in an effort to reduce the amount of time it takes for you to dry your herbs. You will wish later on you had taken the time to do it!

Extractions

When it comes to herbal use for medicines, you may need to extract fluids from the plant. This way, you won't actually be using the plant materials, such as leaves or stems. There are three main methods of extraction you can use. The one you choose can be a personal preference based on need, convenience, and/or the type of herb you are extracting from. It is a good idea to consider all three options before you make a final decision. These options are:

- Infusion
- Decoction
- Tincture

- Infusion

You may hear the term *tisane* used interchangeably with infusion. It is one of the most common and quickest methods of extraction. You will need:

- a small iron pan
- a glass pitcher
- a tea strainer
- a household scale

Don't use pans that are made from aluminum or copper. They can release particles that get into your digestive system. They can also cause the herbs to have a bitter flavor.

Add about a pint of cold water to the pan. Heat until the water boils and then turn off the heat. Add the herb to the water when it is still hot but no longer boiling. Stir gently so the herbs are fully submerged but take care not to damage them.

Allow the plants to remain in the water for 10 minutes. Pour the liquid through the strainer into the glass pitcher. With some herbs, you may need to strain them two or three times due to their potency. Make sure you look into this information for whichever herb you are working with.

Decoction

Another common method of preparing herbs for medicine is decoction. This isn't hard to learn, but many people find that in order to fully master it, they have to practice often. This is a good method to use if you want to make very small amounts of medicine.

Place an ounce of dried herb in a pan with a pint of water and bring it to a boil. Reduce the heat and allow the liquid to continue cooking. Keep an eye on it and remove from the heat when the volume in the pan has been reduced to about ¼ of the original liquid.

Strain it well. Typically, this method is used when you are extracting from bark or roots of herbs. If you need a large amount of the extracted element, this isn't the best method to choose.

Tincture

With this method of extracting from herbs, you will use alcohol instead of water because it is more effective. It draws out more of the valuable medicinal properties than water can. This is why some herbalists will soak the plants in alcohol before they use them.

Don't use methanol or wood alcohol for this method of extraction. Doing so can cause a person to become very ill or even to die. Soak about one ounce of a herb in a pint of alcohol for 8 weeks. Shake the container each day for the first 4 weeks. Then just allow it to sit for the next 4 weeks. Strain well at the end of the 8 week time frame.

Chapter 4
Drying Methods

You have several choices when drying your herbs. Some people have one method they use all the time. For others, it depends on the types of herbs they use. Again, you should explore a few options to decide what works best for you.

No matter which method or methods you plan to use, don't be intimidated! Drying herbs is much easier than you might have imagined. Take some time to learn some basics and you'll be fine.

When Are They Dry?

You must give the herbs sufficient time to completely dry. Plants are completely dry when they are brittle and crumble in your hand with ease. Don't crush the leaves until you are actually ready to use them.

Keep in mind that if the herbs aren't completely dry, they will be susceptible to mold and other problems. Then you will have to throw away the herbs rather than benefitting from your efforts. Give them the time they need to dry completely and you'll be satisfied with the results.

Basic Tips

Before we dive into the actual drying methods, there are some basic tips I would like to share with you. They can help you to gain a solid understanding about why you dry in certain ways.

Drying is the traditional method that was used by early civilizations for preserving herbs. Even though the method is old, it doesn't mean it's not efficient. As the saying goes, you don't have to re-invent the wheel to get results that work!

As mentioned in a previous chapter, always take the time to clean your herbs before you begin to dry them. You don't want to allow dirt and residue to linger.

Never use pesticides to grow your herbs either. Doing so results in the presence of toxins even after you have washed them. Use all-natural methods of growing your herbs for the best overall benefits. Make sure you dry them well after rinsing. You need all of the surface moisture to be removed.

Inspect the herbs you have ready to dry. If there are any signs of damaged or dead foliage, this is the time to remove it. If it lingers it will damage your plants.

Hanging in the Sunlight

You can arrange your herbs in small bundles and tie them together with string. Hang them upside down on the porch in an area where they will get plenty of sunlight. Don't make your bundles too tight or the air won't be able to circulate through them.

Since UV rays can discolor herbs and often reduce their potency, consider covering them. You can do this with a burlap bag that has been cut into pieces. Tie it around the herbs while they are drying and it will allow the sunlight and the air to contact but not damage the herbs.

You can alternatively hang them to dry in your home in a room that is well ventilated. The room also needs to get plenty of sunlight. The attic is a good idea because it is closer to the sun. The basement, on the other hand, won't work due to the limited sunlight. Plus, basements are often damp, and the presence of moisture won't let your herbs dry correctly.

It can take a couple of weeks to successfully dry the herbs this way. After a week, check them each day. If they don't crumble when you pinch them, give it another day and check again.

Air Drying on Screens

If you don't have a porch you can spread the herbs out on screens that you place in your windows. You can even hang them from the ceiling so they can get sunlight without being in the way. Air drying works best for herbs that are typically low moisture. This includes dill, oregano, and rosemary.

Frame Drying

While frame drying your herbs is time consuming, many people feel it gives them the best overall results. It is worth the time and effort they invest in it. Many herbalists use this method, too, as they feel the herbs maintain the most potency through the drying process.

For this method you need a wooden box that is about 3 feet on all sides. The lid should be made from glass. Line the bottom with foil and make sure there is plenty of ventilation. Place the herbs on the foil in a single layer. Secure the lid and make sure you turn the herbs each day until they are dry.

Place the frame in an area where the herbs can get plenty of sunlight each day. Make sure the box is waterproof in case of any rain at night. The rain can cause the herbs to mold. It can take up to 6 weeks for this type of herb drying to be complete.

Microwave

One of the most convenient appliances in the kitchen is the microwave. It is certainly a fast and easy way to heat up foods and to defrost items you wish to cook. Why not use it to help speed up the process of drying herbs?

The right way to do this is to place a single layer of dry leaves between a pair of paper towels. Use heavy-duty paper towels so they don't fall apart. Place the paper towels and herbs into the microwave for 2 minutes on high. Allow them to cool completely.

Check the herbs, and if they aren't completely brittle, give them more heat. 30-second increments are recommended to reduce the risk of scorching. The total time, however, will depend on the wattage of your microwave and the type of herb you're drying.

Oven Drying

If you have a large amount of herbs to dry, the microwave method may be too slow. You can speed things up and get great results with the use of your oven. Place the herbs in a single layer on a cookie sheet. Pre-heat the oven to no more than 200°F. Allow the herbs to sit in the oven for 5 minutes.

When they are completely cool, they should be brittle. If not, you can heat them in the oven again, a few minutes at a time. Once again, the type of herb will influence the amount of time it takes for them to be successfully dried.

Many people like using the oven or the microwave method for drying due to the convenience. It is true you can dry herbs with these methods in a matter of hours versus a matter of weeks. It is especially true for high moisture herbs such as chives, mint, and basil.

However, you must be very careful that you don't scorch the herbs. If you burn them or over-dry them, they aren't going to taste good or offer much nutritional value. Remember, you don't want to *cook* the herbs, just remove the moisture. Oven drying can also lessen the potency of the herbs by about a third.

Dehydrator

You can use a machine called a dehydrator to remove the moisture from your herbs. They can cost from $100 to $400 depending on size, brand, and quality. This is a great tool to use if you can budget for one.

With a dehydrator, you can set the temperature and you can conveniently use the timer so you don't forget about checking them. They also circulate the air which is important for drying the herbs evenly.

For the best results, buy a dehydrator that is round. They come with stacking trays, so you can put a layer of herbs on each of the trays and dehydrate them at the same time. This saves you energy and reduces the overall drying time for all of your herbs.

Salt Drying

While salt drying isn't as popular as other methods, it is still worth mentioning here. You can use non-iodized table salt to dry leaves. Place them in a tray and then sprinkle the salt on top of them. It can take up to 4 weeks for them to dry this way.

Make sure you shake off the extra salt before you package them. It is best to package them in glass jars, rather than plastic bags, if you have used this method.

Freezing

It is also possible to freeze herbs. Many people that live in high-humidity areas use this option. The humidity in the air makes it virtually impossible for them to get their herbs dry enough without the use of extensive heat options.

Once the herbs have been washed, blanch them in water that is boiling. Allow the herbs to remain in the water for 1 minute. Have a container of ice water ready. Move them immediately from the boiling water to the ice bath.

Pat them dry, package them in freezer bags, and put them away. Make sure you remove the air and seal tightly. You should also properly label each bag. We will further discuss labeling in the next chapter.

Chapter 5
How to Store Dried Herbs

Once your herbs are dry, you have one more step to go—packaging for proper storage. It's important not to drop the ball here either, or all your time and effort will have gone to waste.

It is a good idea to think about where you will store the dried herbs before you even get started. You don't need too much room, but you do need a place that is dry and dark. You also don't want to store them in the kitchen, as they can absorb cooking oil or other heavy smells.

Avoid storing them around the laundry room, too, as they can pick up the smell and taste of dryer sheets. The basement, of course, is a poor option due to its dampness. If you live in an area with high humidity, you may even need to run a de-humidifier in the area around the herbs as a precaution.

Jars or Bags

There are some who argue over using glass jars or plastic bags to store your dried herbs. Both methods are used, and truthfully, there doesn't seem to be an advantage of one over the other.

Many consumers like the glass jars because they can recycle them. They know the glass isn't going to harm the environment. Try to use dark colored glass when possible.

Others like the convenience of the bags and they take up less room to store. Bags can be stacked easily.

It really comes down to a personal choice. Avoid the use of metal containers as they can give your herbs a metallic taste. Avoid wood containers as they will absorb moisture.

Regardless of which way you choose, make sure the containers are sealed airtight. For glass jars, this means well-fitted lids. Secure them as tightly as you can. With the bags, remove all the air and make sure the closure is completely secured.

Labeling

Always label your jars or bags of herbs. This is very important because so many of them can look the same. Your label should include:

- Type of herb
- Part of the plant
- Date packaged
- Drying method

Never add more dried herb to a jar until it is completely gone. Otherwise, the older herbs may not be as potent as you want or thought they were. After a year, they start to lose potency.

If you need to store more of an herb, create a second jar for it. Put this second jar behind the first one so you don't accidentally use it first. Once the first jar is all used up, then move and use the second jar.

This is the same type of revolving concept that grocery stores use for their products. They move the oldest item to the front and put the newest to the back. This type of rotation ensures some items don't linger on the shelf longer than others.

Where to Store

You want to store your dried herbs away from sunlight and moisture. Make sure you don't place them in the basement or other location where there can be dampness or drafts. Avoid storing them around the kitchen as the odors from other foods can ruin them!

Never store your herbs anywhere that allows a child or a pet to reach them. While herbs are safe, they can be dangerous in the wrong hands. Some of them are very potent and could make a child or pet ill if directly consumed. Children and pets are both curious, and some herbs smell very good!

If you want to display your herbs, you still won't need too much space. If your area is limited, consider an over-the-door rack. You can place it inside of a hallway closet for example. The jars can fit on the shelves and are easy for you to access. Yet they aren't taking up any additional space in your home.

If you decide to freeze them, it is a good idea to have a small freezer that is separate from your regular one. Perhaps you already have a deep freezer where you store meat and other items. You can allocate a section of it for your herbs.

Check the jars or bags you have filled and stored a few days after you have done so. Inspect them to make sure you don't accidentally pack anything that still had some moisture in it. If you did, take it out of the package or jar and dry the contents again. Then you can repackage them.

If you don't check them, it can be devastating later when you open the package or jar to find mold and other issues. Put a reminder on your calendar to check them the week after packaging. Then check them the week after that. If you don't notice any signs of moisture, you are in the clear!

How Long?

Most herbalists believe you can successfully use herbs that have been dried and stored for up to one year. After that, they will lose their potency and you can't count on them. There are consumers who have used them up to 5 years after packaging and claim good results, but that is a big chance to take.

Herbs may still taste good for up to 5 years, so that is why some people continue to use them. However, the potency of the herbs diminishes with time. The goal of using herbs is adding nutritional and medicinal values. Therefore, it only makes sense to use the herbs when they are still of the best quality.

You wouldn't keep over-the-counter or prescription medications on hand for 5 years, so don't do that with your herbs. This is why the labeling part of the drying and packaging process is so important!

If you find you are coming up on a year and you haven't used all of a given herb, find ways to use it. Find recipes that call for it and try them out! You and your family will love the change in the menu, as we get tired of eating the same dishes often.

You can also offer some of the remaining herbs to your friends or family in the last few months of the year. Perhaps they haven't tried drying their own herbs but they are interested. Tasting yours can be the incentive they need to try it on their own! Plus, sharing with others is a better option than tossing unused herbs out.

Chapter 6
Common Mistakes to Avoid

While drying your own herbs is a learning experience, you don't want to learn certain things the hard way. By avoiding these common mistakes, you will reap the benefits from your efforts and reduce the risk of spoiling your herbs.

#1—Using herbs as a replacement for medical care.

While you can use herbs for various minor ailments, you shouldn't rely on them instead of medical care. For example, you may find the use of certain herbs reduces the pain and inflammation of your arthritis. You still need to keep your regular appointment with your doctor, however, and you should disclose your use of herbs.

It is fine to tell the doctor that you would rather rely on these herbs than to take prescription medications. That is your right, but you still need to get annual checkups and other medical care.

#2—Ignoring quality.

Be selective when it comes to the plant you choose. If they aren't healthy, they won't be able to provide you with nutritional or medicinal value. It is important to understand that not all plants are the same.

Starting out with a growing plant for your herbs—instead of seeds—is a common practice. Just make sure you have evaluated the plants to ensure they are healthy. If you notice any problems, it is best not to buy them.

#3—Using chemicals.

Avoid using pesticides or chemical fertilizers to help your plants grow. You'll want the herbs to remain as natural as possible. The only way to make that happens is to ensure they are grown in the best conditions.

Use organic soil and use natural methods to eliminate bugs and other entities that could ruin your plants. Take the time to weed them and to remove dead foliage regularly. If you allow it to linger, it will zap the healthy plant of the nutrients it needs to grow.

#4—Getting the wrong amount of water or light.

The right amount of water and sunlight is essential for herbs to grow as they should. The soil should be wet when you touch it but not soaked. Too much water can increase the chances of mold and harmful bacteria growing. Not enough water can result in a stunted plant.

Herbs need sunlight to grow, so make sure you place them in a windowsill or grow them outdoors where they get plenty. If you notice some herbs in your window garden are doing better than others, rotate the plants. The additional sunlight can be good for them.

Don't plant outdoors in areas where there is too much shade. Before you plant, evaluate the amount of shade and sunlight the area gets throughout the day. On hotter days, your plants may require more water than usual, so pay attention to how they are doing in various weather conditions.

#5—Overcrowding.

Give your herbs plenty of room to grow. Not only do they grow taller, but most need to grow wider as well. Limiting conditions may cause a plant to grow weak or sickly, as it must adapt to the space it's been given. With healthy plants, less is more and you will get the best yield for that particular herb.

#6—Seeding.

If you prune and harvest your herbs regularly, they won't seed. The seeding process signals the end of their growth. By pruning and cutting, you encourage the plants to continue to grow. Then you can prolong the cycle of growing and harvesting them.

#7—Not drying the herbs completely.

One of the most common mistakes with drying herbs is not drying them completely. Take your time with any of the drying methods and ensure they are completely dry. Don't forget to check them after a few days of packaging. If they aren't dry, this is the time to take them out and dry them more.

#8—Not packing them properly.

Don't fall short at the last step—packaging. You need to label your herbs so you know what they are and how long you've had them. Use airtight bags or airtight jars. Store away from moisture and sunlight.

#9—Not learning about your particular herbs.

It is a huge pitfall not to learn about the particular herbs you are going to grow. The more you know about the best growing methods, harvesting techniques, drying practices, etc., the easier it is going to be.

This is also why you should only start with two or three herbs at first. As you become more skilled with the process, you can consider adding more to your garden. Too much at once, though, can make you feel overwhelmed.

#10—Rushing the process.

While your days may be very busy, carve out some time for your herbs to get started. The initial steps will be the most time consuming. Then it is just a matter of keeping them watered and ensuring they get enough sunlight.

Pay attention to when your herbs need to be pruned, too. If you ignore this, it will slow down growth and limit the quality of the herbs.

Allocate plenty of time for harvesting and for drying. The herbs aren't going to work around your schedule, so you have to be ready for them. You need to give the drying process all the time it requires, and it can't be hurried.

#11—Not even trying.

Giving up before you even get started is a guaranteed failure! Too many people assume they can't do this so they don't even try. However, by following step-by-step, you'll be able to get results.

How to Dry Herbs

You have the ability to grow your own herbs, to dry them, and to access them whenever you'd like. Use what you learn in this book to help you get started. Give yourself credit for moving forward and experimenting. See what works well for you and create a plan of action that keeps you motivated.

Chapter 7
Common Herbs to Dry

There are too many herbs to list them all here, but you can dry whatever you would like to use. Here is a list of the most common herbs to consider drying. There is no right or wrong types to work with. Think about what you want from a nutritional medicinal standpoint and go from there.

Antioxidants

One of the reasons people use herbs is the powerful antioxidants they contain. These antioxidants help to naturally flush toxins and free radicals from the body. As a result you are healthier inside and out.

The herbs offering the highest levels of antioxidants are:

- Allspice
- Cloves
- Cinnamon
- Lemon Balm
- Marjoram
- Oregano
- Peppermint
- Rosemary
- Saffron
- Thyme

More Specific Benefits

There are some herbs you may wish to dry and use for specific benefits. As you learn about the potential benefits, it may encourage you to grow and harvest them. Here is a list of effects that may interest you.

Have Younger and Healthier Skin

Many men and women are looking for the fountain of youth! They don't want to see fine lines and wrinkles when they look in the mirror. Protecting your skin cells is the key to staying younger looking naturally.

Italian spices can be added to foods you prepare. Basil is the most common Italian spice used in foods. Not only does it taste great, but it also helps to protect the skin cells. The powerful antioxidants found in basil can also help the body fight off harmful germs.

Basil can also help reduce the risk of serious health problems. This includes Alzheimer's disease, various types of cancer, heart disease, and osteoporosis. These are all health problems that can reduce your overall quality of life, so fighting against them is important.

Promote Healing

As we get older, it can take our bodies longer to heal from cuts. This can increase the risk of bacterial infections. Harmful bacteria in the body can also result in a sore throat, strep throat, or even pneumonia over time.

Thyme is a powerful herb that can help promote healing. It attacks the harmful bacteria but won't destroy the good bacteria in your body. Thyme can also help to reduce inflammation and throat pain. It can aid the body in healing cuts and scrapes faster.

Reduce Inflammation

For many individuals, chronic pain has become part of life. However, it limits their mobility and quality of life in many regards. Sage is an herb that can help to reduce inflammation and to slow down the aging of the body.

Such inflammation is often associated with asthma, various forms of arthritis, and the hardening of arteries. Adding some sage to the foods you eat regularly can be a natural way to help reduce the inflammation and the pain associated with these conditions.

Sleep Better

When your body is able to sleep well, you will be amazed how much better you feel. Your mind and your body need sleep to feel refreshed and happy. Tossing and turning all night is uncomfortable and makes you feel awful in the morning.

Using sleep aids can leave you feeling groggy and foggy in the morning. Marjoram is an herb that can naturally help you to sleep easier and better.

Marjoram is best used as an extract. It is very powerful, so you would only need to use about 5 drops of this oil in the bathtub. Get into the routine of doing so before you sleep and see how much better you feel in the morning!

Boost Your Immune System

Prevention is a key part of a healthy lifestyle. Don't wait until you don't feel well to take action. Oregano is an exceptional herb to consider if you would like to boost your immune system. It can help reduce the risk of health concerns due to viruses, bacteria, or free radicals.

Oregano is often used as a natural antibiotic and a natural antifungal agent. It can help clear up a yeast infection or nail fungus issue.

Maintain Heart Health

A healthy heart is important at any age, but it becomes more important as we get older. Heart disease is the leading cause of death for both men and women in the USA. Ginger is a great choice when it comes to reducing the risk of heart problems.

Ginger has been proven to help reduce the risk of clogged arteries. That is a huge factor in preventing heart attacks. Ginger also helps prevent fungus and bacteria problems from affecting the heart. It can also boost the immune system. Furthermore, ginger is a natural way to reduce bad cholesterol levels, known as LDL.

Improve Digestion

When the body isn't digesting food correctly, it can make you very uncomfortable. You may suffer from acid reflux, gas, or bloating. None of these effects are appealing. Allspice has a unique taste that is very good and can be added to a variety of foods or used as a tea.

This herb is a natural way to improve overall digestion. It can also assist your digestive tract. It reduces problems with acid due to the way it activates digestion. You can add allspice to your meats, vegetables, soups and broths.

Allspice can also help to regulate blood sugar levels. It can be helpful for regulating cholesterol, too. It adds plenty of flavor to foods but also plenty of value to your overall health.

Fight Bacteria

If we could see the bacteria and germs all around, it would be a nightmare. We rely on our immune system to help us stay as healthy as possible. Cinnamon helps to fight harmful bacteria. It can even prevent serious health problems that would require antibiotics or more powerful forms of treatment.

Our muscles and joints can start to be less mobile as we get older. Cinnamon can help to reduce such problems, as it has anti-inflammatory compounds. It can also help reduce the risks of tooth decay, gum disease, E. coli, and urinary tract infections (UTIs).

Prevent Cancer

The battle against cancer is very serious and costs many lives. Preventing cancer should be high on your list when taking care of your body. Turmeric is a wonderful root that can help you do just that. It also helps lower the risk of Alzheimer's disease.

Turmeric contains *curcumin*—it is what gives the root its yellow coloring. Curcumin helps prevent DNA mutations which can result in cancer.

Achieve a Healthy Mind and Body

It seems that the miracle herb is cloves. It is very powerful for a variety of reasons. It can help reduce pain in muscles and joints and is full of powerful antioxidants to boost your immune system and to fight off free radicals.

Eugenol is found in cloves, which is a type of mild and natural anesthesia. It can be used to reduce the pain of a sore throat, irritated gums, or toothache. Cloves can also offer relief to those who suffer from chronic breathing issues such as bronchitis and asthma.

Cloves is a well-known anti-bacteria and anti-fungal option, too. In reality, you just can't go wrong with the use of cloves. There is so much it can protect against!

Conclusion

Herbs have been used for centuries in many cultures for both nutritional value and medicinal purposes. As modern medicine evolved, they became less common. However, many people want to get back to the basics. They don't want to take chemicals all the time or suffer from the side effects of prescription medications.

Over-the-counter and prescription medications can be expensive for consumers. And for those who need ongoing medication, it can be a huge burden on their budgets. Feeling better but in an affordable way is important.

When you grow and dry your own herbs, it is much cheaper than anything you can purchase. If you grow perennial types of herbs, you will have a one-time expense to get started. Then they will grow again and again, year after year for you. As long as you harvest them correctly and care for them with water and sunlight, they will grow well.

You are also in complete control over their quality. Never assume that bottled herbs you buy or even those available at a farmer's market have been grown under the best conditions.

Research shows that the majority of dried herbs for sale aren't organic. They have been grown with the help of pesticides that contain harmful chemicals. Those that are certified as organic cost significantly more.

When you buy dried herbs in bottles, they have been irradiated in most cases. This means they have been exposed to a type of gamma radiation. It is done to destroy any traces of pathogens. However, this process can also reduce the overall potency of the herbs.

The information we have access to today suggests that by taking better care of your body early in life, you can reduce potential health problems later on. Who wants to live to be 100, but be so sick that they can't enjoy their longevity? The goal should be to enjoy those golden years and to be as healthy as possible.

Drying your own herbs can provide you with the means to prevent and to fight various types of health concerns. Prevention is a big piece of the health puzzle that is sadly often overlooked. Many people don't worry about the state of their bodies until they become ill or are diagnosed with serious problems such as cancer or heart disease.

It is our responsibility to take care of our bodies. Don't blame genetics and don't leave it to chance. Using these herbs can be the simple and the effective way to improve your health now and to avoid serious health concerns in the future.

Identify a couple of herbs that can assist you with your particular needs. Take the time to learn about what benefits they offer and the best way to use them. Find out how to grow them using the most effective and most efficient methods. At the same time, learn how to harvest them successfully.

Evaluate several of the drying methods so you can choose one that works for your needs. Keep in mind that some types of herbs do better with one drying method than another. Your personal preferences also play a role in what you do.

Make sure the herbs are completely dry in order to use them later. Place them into glass jars or airtight bags and label them. Then you can reach for the herbs when you need them without any problems or hassles.

You are going to open up many great opportunities for yourself and your family by growing and drying your own herbs. The preventative care will reduce your chance of illness and help you to enjoy life to the fullest!

Did you Like "How to Dry Herbs"?

Before you go, I'd like to say thank you so much for purchasing my book.

I know you could have picked from dozens of books on this subject, but you took a chance with mine, and I'm truly grateful for that.

So, once again, a big thanks for downloading this book and reading all the way to the end—I truly appreciate it.

Now I'd like to ask for a small favor if you don't mind:

Would you be so kind as to take a minute of your time and leave a review for this book on Amazon?

This feedback will help me continue to write the kind of books that help you get results. And if you loved it, then please feel free to let me know! :)

More Books By Ella Marie:

Baking Soda Cure: Discover the Amazing Power and Health Benefits of Baking Soda, its History and Uses For Cooking, Cleaning, and Curing Ailments

Essential Oils For Beginners: The Little Known Secrets to Essential Oils and Aromatherapy for Weight Loss, Beauty and Healing

Yoga For Beginners: The Ultimate Beginner Yoga Guide to Lose Weight, Relieve Stress and Tone Your Body With Yoga

Leptin Resistance: The Ultimate Leptin Resistance Diet Guide For Weight Loss Including Delicious Recipes And How to Overcome Leptin Resistance Naturally

DASH Diet For Weight Loss: The Ultimate Beginner Dash Diet Guide For Weight Loss, Lower Blood Pressure, and Better Health Including Delicious Dash Diet Recipes

Mindfulness For Beginners: 25 Easy Mindfulness Exercises To Help You Live In The Present Moment, Conquer Anxiety And Stress, And Have A Fulfilling Life with Mindfulness Meditation

Vegan Slow Cooker: The Ultimate Vegan Slow Cooker Cookbook Including 39 Easy & Delicious Vegan Slow Cooker Recipes For Breakfast, Lunch & Dinner!

Herbal Antibiotics: 56 Little Known Natural and Holistic Remedies To Help Cure And Prevent Bacterial Illnesses

Paleo Slow Cooker: 35 Easy, Delicious, and Healthy Paleo Slow Cooker Recipes For Busy People

Mason Jar Meals: 38 Little Known, Easy, Healthy & Delicious Mason Jar Recipes for Busy, On-the-Go People

Printed in Great Britain
by Amazon